NATIONAL WILDLIFE FEDERATION®
Book of Endangered Species

Rare, Vulnerable, and Endangered Species of the World

Written by Beth Lyons
Cover and interior illustrations by Ken Maestas

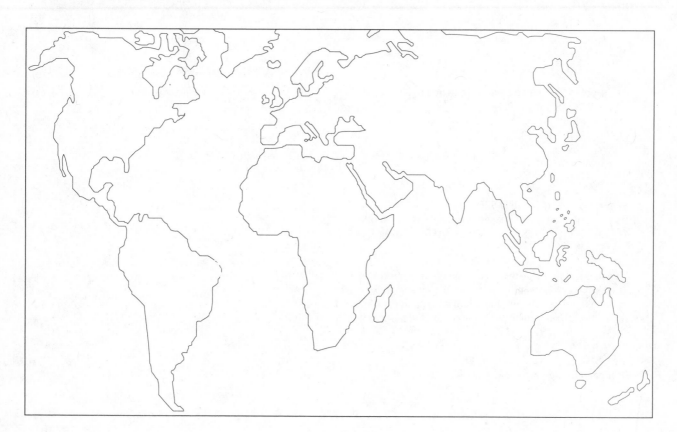

Published in the United States of America by
EARTHBOOKS, INCORPORATED
7000 North Broadway
Building One Suite 103
Denver, Colorado   80221
Steven W. Schmidt, President

BOOK OF ENDANGERED SPECIES
Rare, Vulnerable, and Endangered Species of the World
© 1991 EARTHBOOKS, INCORPORATED, Denver, Colorado

ISBN 1-877731-17-X

Printed in Boulder, Colorado, USA

TABLE OF CONTENTS

AYE–AYE

Some people once thought the aye-aye (EYE-eye) had special powers. No one dared to harm it. Other people were just plain afraid of the aye-aye. They believed that if they touched one, they would die soon. If an aye-aye came to a village, the people would kill it or drive it away.

Today this animal is almost extinct. It lives only in Madagascar—and there are only a few of them in the wild. A few others have been brought to a special reserve. This place is on an island near Madagascar.

The aye-aye looks like an odd assortment of several animals. Can you see any features that are like other animals? You might say that it has a bushy tail like a fox. Or ears like a bat. Or long fingers like a monkey. Some people even think it looks like a weird squirrel. In any case, this odd animal also has an odd name. The name aye-aye comes from a cry the native people made when they were frightened by the animal.

As with many animals, the aye-aye has certain features for a reason. Take those long, thin fingers, for example. Each one has a curved claw that is used as a hook. The middle finger is longer than the rest. This is used for finding and digging out food.

Let's follow an aye-aye as it hunts for food. The aye-aye lives in trees in a forest. It eats insects and plants. So let's say it comes across a log. There might be some tasty insects inside. The aye-aye taps the log with its middle finger. Then it puts its huge ear next to the log and listens. If it hears anything, it uses its long, sharp teeth to chew through the wood. Then comes that middle finger again. It hooks the food and pulls it out of the log.

The main problem for the aye-aye now is that forests are being cut down. This ruins the animal's home and its source of food. The future does not look good for the aye-aye. The reserve is trying to save it, but it may be too late.

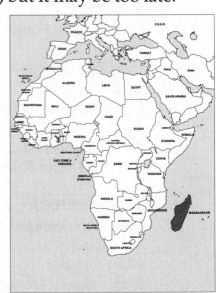

Color: Dark brown body with white flecks; yellow eyes rimmed with black.

WALIA IBEX

If you ever want to see a walia ibex (EYE-beks), you'd better hurry. In fact, you would have to take a trip to Africa. Even then, you might not be able to see this rare wild goat. There are only a few hundred left. And the only place you can see them now is in the Simien Mountains of Ethiopia.

Humans are the main reason the walia ibex is so rare. This animal has few natural enemies. If it lived on the plains, it would be killed by leopards and hyenas. But it lives among rocky cliffs, high in the mountains. Few enemies can reach it there. That may be the only reason this animal is not extinct today.

Local tribes have hunted the walia ibex for years. They wanted its hide, its meat, and its horns. The horns made valuable drinking cups. Then some people realized what was happening to the ibex. The government passed laws about killing it. But people paid no attention to the laws. They continued killing the animal. This became even easier when repeating rifles were available.

The walia ibex is now protected in the Simien Mountains National Park. This area has many steep cliffs and grassy ledges. Here the ibex can find food and shelter. There are many places for it to hide from enemies. And by law, it cannot be harmed there by hunters.

The ibex is well suited for living in a rocky place. It has thin, sturdy legs. Its hooves are divided into two toes. This gives the ibex good footing along rocks and ledges. The male walia ibex has long curved horns.

The future of the walia ibex is uncertain. There are so few left today that it could become extinct. The government of Ethiopia will have to watch and protect this animal very carefully.

Color: Brownish-gray coat with grayish legs and dark brown or black stripes. The horns are gray.

WHITE-NECKED ROCKFOWL

The white-necked rockfowl not only can fly, it also can leap. It has very long legs, which propel it off the ground.

The rockfowl is also called a bald crow. This is because it has no feathers on its head. Instead, it has bright yellow on its cheeks and upper neck. Everywhere else it is covered with feathers. They are brownish-gray on top of its back and white below.

The nests of these birds are found in odd places. Some are attached to the sides of steep vertical rocks or are found in caves. Others may be found clinging to the underside of rocks that jut out. These nests are cup-shaped and made of mud. Why do you think the nests stay attached to the rocks?

The rockfowl eats amphibians and insects. When the rockfowl has young to feed, it will eat its food and let it partly digest. Then it vomits up the food and gives it to the baby birds.

Some of these rare birds are found in the forests of West Africa. Others have been raised in a Frankfurt, Germany, zoo.

There are two main reasons that the rockfowl has become rare. People have destroyed its forest habitat by cutting down trees. They have also taken these birds from their nests and have sold them to make money. Collectors pay a lot of money for rare, unusual birds. That is why some rockfowl are being raised in zoos like the one in Frankfurt. It is one of the few ways left to protect this bird.

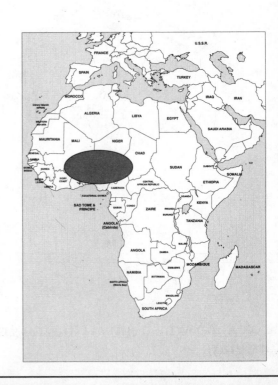

Color: Bright yellow for the cheeks and upper neck; brownish-gray on top of back; and white on the chest.

GOLIATH FROG

Perhaps you have heard the story of David and Goliath. Goliath was a giant, so the name goliath is used to mean anything that is huge. In this case, goliath refers to a frog. And compared to most frogs, the goliath frog is a real giant. It is almost a foot long. It is the largest frog in the world. Compare that with the smallest frog, which is only about 1/2 inch long. That's quite a difference!

The goliath frog is an animal called an amphibian (am-FIB-ee-uhn). An amphibian spends part of its life in the water and part on land. Like most frogs, the goliath has long and strong back legs. This helps the frog leap great distances. Notice the webbed feet on those legs. Do you think this frog is a good swimmer?

Many people in Africa believe that the large thighbone of the goliath frog has magical powers and can bring good luck, sort of like people in North America who believe that a rabbit's foot can bring good luck.

The goliath frog is found in tropical Africa. It lives in deep pools in fast-flowing mountain streams. To produce its young, the frog needs clean, clear streams. But this has been a problem because people pollute the streams, and without clean water the goliath frog may have a hard time reproducing.

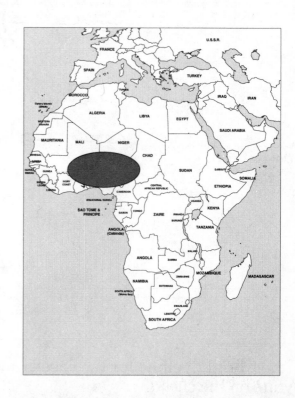

Color: Brownish-green.

SLOTH BEAR

The sloth bear is slowly disappearing. Long ago it was found all over India and nearby areas. Today it lives in a small part of India and Sri Lanka. People are cutting down the forests where it lives. They are making room for highways and buildings. This not only destroys the bear's habitat, but it also kills food the bear needs to eat.

People have harmed this bear in other ways. They have hunted it for its fur and meat, even though this is against the law. They have stolen bear cubs to tame. They turn the cubs into "dancing bears" that work with jugglers in the streets. People have also killed the bear when it has eaten their crops. They forget that when an animal's habitat is destroyed, it has to eat something, even if that something is good crops.

The name sloth bear for this animal is not quite correct. At one time people thought it was related to the sloth of South America. The sloth is an animal with long, hook-like claws that allow it to hang from tree branches. The sloth bear has claws much like the sloth's, but it is still called a bear.

The sloth bear uses its long front claws mostly for climbing and for eating. These claws are very handy for cracking open an anthill, a beehive, or a mound that may be as hard as a rock. This bear eats mostly insects (ants, bees, and termites), as well as honey, fruit, and flowers.

It is the bear's snout, though, that really helps it collect food. Let's say the sloth bear comes across an anthill. First it blows all the dust away. Then, with its lips and its long, flat tongue, it shapes a tube. It sucks up the ants like it's using a vacuum cleaner!

The country of India is working to protect the sloth bear. It is providing parks and refuges for it. It is also trying to keep the bear's natural habitat, the forest, from being totally destroyed as well.

Color: Black body with cream-colored mark in shape of a "V" on chest and a cream-colored snout.

SNUB-NOSED MONKEY

Many people in the United States are concerned about killing animals for their fur. These animals include the mink, the fox, the otter, and others. Maybe you even have an opinion about this. In some Asian countries in the past, other animals were killed for their fur. One of these was the golden monkey, which is also called the snub-nosed monkey.

Years ago in China and Tibet, the fur of the golden monkey was very valuable. Huge cloaks were made of the fur. But only certain high officials could wear these fur cloaks.

People paid a large price for the monkey fur. Because of this, there was constant hunting going on. The monkey was either shot or trapped. Soon it became very scarce. It is only because of strict laws that this monkey even exists at all today. Fortunately, shooting and trapping of this animal are strictly forbidden in China.

The snub-nosed monkey has this name for a good reason. "Snub-nosed" means that the nose is short and turned up at the end. The tip of the monkey's nose almost touches its forehead.

This monkey lives in the high mountain ranges of China and Tibet. It is one of the few kinds of monkeys that <u>does</u> live in a cold climate. Most monkeys live in warm, tropical places. The snub-nosed monkey is even called the "snow monkey." Its habitat is covered with snow about half of the year. This is when it goes to the lower valleys to look for food.

Home for the snub-nosed monkey is in trees. This is very handy because it eats leaves, buds, fruit, and bamboo shoots. Monkeys that live in trees have fairly long tails. The tail helps them balance on tree branches, and it helps to slow them down as they leap from branch to branch.

16

Color: Black upper body with white hairs; lower body is golden.

CHINESE ALLIGATOR

The alligator has a great disguise. It can lurk in a swamp or muddy river and look like a floating log. Its gray-black hide blends in very well with its surroundings.

The Chinese alligator is much like the American alligator. It is shaped like a lizard with a thicker body and tail. It lives in the lower Yangtze River Valley in China. The American alligator is found in the southeastern United States, especially Florida.

People sometimes confuse alligators and crocodiles. They are from the same family. But frankly, most people don't want to get close enough to really be able to tell the difference. The difference is that when the crocodile's mouth is closed, a big tooth shows, but when the alligator closes its mouth the tooth cannot be seen.

Speaking of snouts, let's look at the alligator's eating habits. First of all, the alligator rarely eats humans. It does bite and can cause real harm. But once the alligator's mouth is shut, a person can hold the jaws closed with bare hands. (That's if the person can get the jaws closed!) The alligator feeds on snails, mussels, and fish. The larger alligators will attack small dogs, pigs, or even cattle. First it drags the animal under water to drown it. Then it tears it to pieces. The alligator doesn't chew its food. It swallows it whole or in pieces.

Humans are probably the worst enemy of the alligator. In the past, people killed and skinned the alligator for its hide. This is because the skin is very tough. When it is made into leather, it is beautiful and lasts a long time. People loved having alligator purses, belts, and shoes. The alligator was also killed for its meat and because people were afraid of it. The Chinese alligator is now very close to extinction. Little has been done to protect it, although a few may exist in zoos.

Color: Gray- black.

SIBERIAN WHITE CRANE

You might think that a bird living in the tundra of Siberia would be safe from extinction. After all, the tundra is a very cold region where few people and other animals live. The Siberian tundra is in the far northern part of Asia. It is near the Arctic Ocean.

The Siberian white crane migrates, or flies to other places, though. It does this during the winter months when the ground and water are frozen solid in Siberia and there is nothing to eat. Some cranes go to places in and around India. Others fly to Afghanistan and southern Russia.

Besides humans, who sometimes shoot it on its breeding grounds, the crane has few enemies. Herds of reindeer scare the crane from its nest or accidentally destroy nests by stepping on them.

The crane is being protected in two important ways. A wintering area in India has been declared a bird sanctuary. The other way is a "foster parents plan." In 1976, a project was started to use common cranes, which nest south of the Urals and winter at Lake Perishan in Iran, to take care of baby Siberian white cranes.

The Siberian white crane is a large and beautiful bird. It is pure white except for its face and bill and its legs and feet. It is very graceful when it flies, flapping its wings slowly and stretching its neck to full length. Its long, pointed beak can poke around under water for plants and fish.

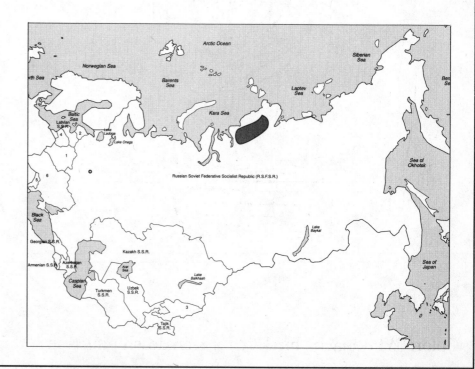

Color: White body; brick-red face; reddish-pink legs and feet.

INDIAN PYTHON

The python has always been a popular snake in zoos, reptile houses, and circus shows. These are probably the only places that most people would be able to see this giant, 20-foot snake. (Measure off 20 feet and you'll see why this snake is called "giant." Twenty feet may be longer than your living room.)

The popularity of this snake is one reason it is endangered. People have also hunted the python for its beautiful, tough skin. This skin can be made into many items like belts, purses, and luggage. Python meat is also highly prized in some countries.

It's too bad for the python, then, that it is not a dangerous snake—at least not to humans. And humans are its main enemy. The python is not poisonous, nor does it attack humans. Fortunately, the python is now protected by law. It cannot be hunted for any reason.

The Indian python lives in India, of course, and countries near there. Its habitat is a thick rain forest. Here is where the python finds its food. A large python will eat animals about the size of a house rat. This snake has even been known to eat leopards!

The python kills its prey by squeezing it to death, so it is called a constrictor. It wraps its body around the animal and tightens its coils. This causes the victim to stop breathing. It also stops the heartbeat. When the victim is dead, the python swallows it whole. It may then take several days for this food to be digested by the python.

Like most snakes, the python lays eggs--up to 50 at a time. The female python cannot warm the eggs with her own body, but she can move them toward the sun or into the shade to control the temperature of the eggs.

The python will need to be watched carefully. Although it is protected by law, the law does little to protect the snake's habitat. As people destroy more forests, they will continue to kill the many animals that live there.

Color: Dark brown and yellow pattern on tan background.

23

HAIRY-NOSED WOMBAT

What animal looks like a small bear, digs burrows like a badger, and has a pouch? It could be either the common wombat or the hairy-nosed wombat. And what's the difference between these two? The common wombat is not endangered; the hairy-nosed one is. As you may have also guessed, the hairy-nosed wombat has just that—a hairy nose. Well, actually, its whole face is pretty hairy. And it has plenty of hair on the rest of its body, too.

The hairy-nosed wombat lives on the hot, dry plains of southeastern Australia. Its long, strong front claws help it to dig deep burrows. This is where the wombat spends its days, trying to stay cool. Then it goes out at night in search of food. It doesn't seem to mind the dark because it has poor eyesight anyway. Good thing it has keen senses of smell and hearing, though.

Like the kangaroo, the female wombat has a pouch. This is where she carries her young. She has only one baby each year. But sometimes there are droughts (DROWTS), or very little rainfall, in Australia. Then the female does not produce any young at all.

The wombat will never have to worry about having too little fiber in its diet. It gets a lot of it by eating herbs, grasses, roots, and fungi. It has teeth that are well suited for eating these plants. In addition to regular teeth, it also has two gnawing teeth. These two teeth grow all the time. All that gnawing and chewing keep these teeth from getting too long.

Wombats die from diseases and some starve during dry spells. Humans are not much of a problem, although some wombats are killed by cars and trucks. The wombat is not popular with ranchers, though. It eats food the ranchers want to give to their livestock.

The wombat is now protected by law in Australia. Most of them live in their natural habitat in a national park there.

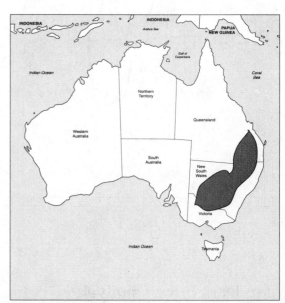

Color: Black-brown body.

TUATARA

In New Zealand, they take their tuatara (too-ah-TAR-ah) very seriously. In fact, there are about 30 small islands that are like "tuatara paradise." In these places it is against the law to capture or kill a tuatara. New Zealand is the only place in the world that has tuataras. They are now extinct everywhere else.

The tuatara has been around for a very long time. It is even called a "living fossil." That's because it has survived without much change for about 200 million years. It lived on Earth even before the Rocky Mountains were formed. Now that's an old species!

The modern tuatara has ancestors known as beak-heads. They came in many shapes and sizes. Some grew to be six feet long. When the dinosaurs ruled the land, many beak-heads died off. But in the end, you see which reptile survived.

The tuatara is not exactly a pretty sight. It looks somewhat like a fat lizard. This scaly reptile has bony plates along its neck and back. The name tuatara means "spine-back." It refers to these bony plates. The name comes from the Maoris (MOU-reez). They are natives of New Zealand.

Home for the tuatara is a burrow in the ground. Sometimes, though, the tuatara takes over a ground hole that has been dug by a bird. When this happens, the tuatara just moves in and forces the bird out. It occasionally eats lizards and the eggs or young of a bird called the petrel.

Rats are the main enemy of the tuatara. But in the "tuatara paradise" of New Zealand, many have been removed. This has allowed the tuatara population to grow. There are probably 100,000 or more living today. Some of these may live to be 100 years old. This does not mean, though, that the tuatara is safe from extinction. It must still be closely watch and protected. After all, it is one of the oldest species on Earth.

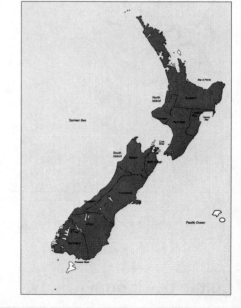

Color: Tan or dull green body with white spots on scales and brown lines on sides.

NUMBAT

The numbat is also known as a banded anteater. But it doesn't look much like the anteater you may know about. It looks more like a squirrel with stripes or a rat with a bushy tail.

The numbat also doesn't feed much on ants. It is really a termite-eater. It spends most of its time looking for these insects in dead trees. Since termites eat wood, the numbat makes its home where there are many trees. When it finds a dead log, it digs rapidly with its front claws. And where there are dead logs, there are usually lots of termites. The numbat then puts its long, sticky tongue into the termite nest to get its food. It doesn't chew this food. It swallows the termites whole, along with soil and bits of bark.

The colored bands on the back of the numbat are its disguise. They help it hide from its enemies. When the numbat lies on dark tree branches, it can hardly be seen.

Although the numbat is a marsupial, it does not have a pouch. Maybe you have heard of other marsupials, such as the kangaroo. The kangaroo has a pouch where it carries its young. The female numbat carries her young on the underside of her body. She may have up to four babies a year.

Southern and southwestern Australia is the home of the numbat. This animal was once found in New South Wales as well. But people and nature have killed off many of the numbats. Brush fires and droughts are natural enemies, along with foxes and dogs. People have cut down many trees where the numbat lives. They wanted to use the land for farming. This, of course, destroys the numbat's habitat. When there are no trees, there are no termites, and the numbat then has nothing to eat.

People in Australia are being more careful about clearing land for farming. They know that the numbat is an endangered animal. They want to keep it from becoming extinct. People are also providing places where the numbat can raise its young without being harmed by people or other animals.

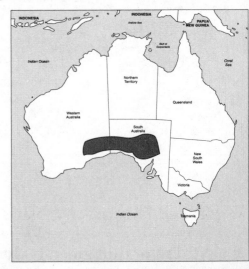

Color: Red-brown body; black toward the tail with white or yellowish stripes on the lower back; front and back legs and belly are red-brown; black stripe on side of head from nose to ear.

NEW ZEALAND SHORE PLOVER

The name plover can be said two ways—(PLUH-vuhr) or (PLOH-vuhr). It refers to a group of small shore birds. There are many kinds of plovers throughout the world. The New Zealand shore plover is one of the rarest, though. It is found on only one tiny island that is part of New Zealand. This is South East Island, one of the Chatham Islands.

The plover was once found all over New Zealand. So why is it now almost extinct? Commercial collectors, people who collect birds to sell, caught too many of them and almost wiped them out. They took the bird from its natural habitat and sold it or kept it for themselves. Sometimes the bird was not handled carefully and it died. Or it could not adapt to a different habitat and died that way. The New Zealand shore plover is now fully protected by law. South East Island is a preserve for it.

The shore plover builds its nest of grass on the ground among rocks and pebbles. This works really well for hiding the eggs. The eggs are greenish-gray with dark spots. They blend in very well with the pebbles around them. The plover always makes its nest on the ground, never in a tree.

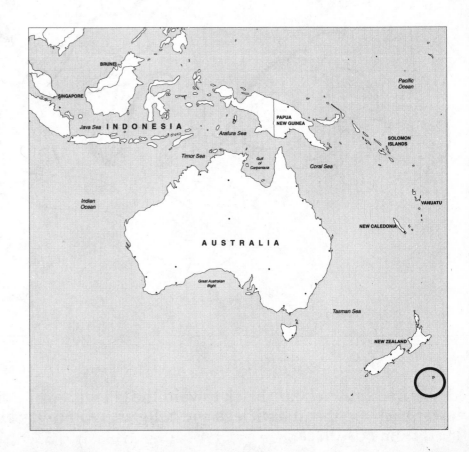

Color: Brown upper body with black throat and front of face; white back of head; white breast and orange bill darkening to black at the tip.

PYRENEAN DESMAN

The Pyrenean (peer-uh-NEE-un) desman is an animal with several talents. It can burrow, it can swim, and it can use its snout as a kind of snorkel in the water. This animal is from the mole family, so it lives in a hole, or burrow. But unlike most moles, it has webbed toes on its hind paws. This helps it move underwater.

The desman is a great swimmer. The surface of its hairy coat is water-repellent. The hairs trap a thin layer of air under them. This helps the desman in two ways. Since the animal has no fat under its skin, the air keeps its body warm. It acts as a layer of insulation. The air also helps the desman stay afloat. When it has been underwater, it can pop to the surface like a cork.

Then there's the desman's snout—now there's a nose! The animal uses this snout like an elephant uses its trunk. It waves it around to smell and feel for food.

The Pyrenean desman gets that name because it lives in the Pyrenees (PEER-uh-neez) Mountains. These mountains are between Spain and France. This animal lives in and around mountain streams. Most of its food comes from the water—insects, crustaceans, and small fish. Since the desman itself is only about four or five inches long, it has to find very tiny fish to eat.

The main enemy of the desman is humans. Humans pollute the water where the animals live. The pollution kills not only the desman but also the food it eats. The desman is protected by law. People cannot kill it outright. But they are still killing it by destroying its habitat.

Color: Reddish-brown body.

CHAMOIS

The chamois (SHAM-ee) is a bit of a daredevil. It can leap across icy cliffs and gallop down steep, rocky hills. It can walk along a narrow ledge without missing a step. What is it that makes this animal such a great mountain climber? The answer is in its hooves.

The soles of the chamois's hooves are soft and elastic. They can bend on the rocky ground. The edges of the hooves are harder. They have a rim to keep the chamois from slipping. These hooves can also dig into the snow and ground to hold even better. Being able to move quickly helps to protect this animal. It can easily run away from its enemies—eagles, wolves, and bears.

The chamois is related to the mountain goat. Both animals live high in the mountains or in valleys between mountains. The chamois is found in central and south Europe, Asia Minor, and Caucasus Mountains. A sub- species of the chamois is strictly protected in the Abrazzo National Park.

For part of the year, the chamois may move in a herd. In the fall, the herd moves to lower elevations and returns to the alpine, higher elevations, in the spring.

Some of the male chamois fight with each other. This is mainly to see which one is superior. The animals have short horns that curve backward, which they use to butt each other. These horns can also tear the opponent's hide. The fighters tend to go for the throat or chest. The stronger animal will usually cause the weaker one to back off or run away.

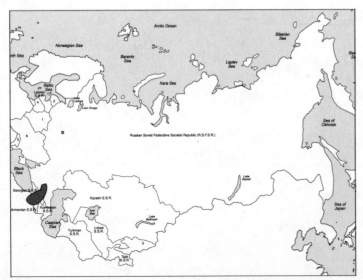

Color: Golden brown with black tail and horns; head is golden with black band around the eyes.

SPANISH IMPERIAL EAGLE

If you saw this eagle up close, it would probably look very fierce and bold. Or if you saw an eagle soar high in the sky, it might look majestic. The truth is, few people are lucky enough to see this eagle at all. It is a very rare and endangered bird of prey.

The Spanish imperial eagle, like other eagles, is called a bird of prey because it hunts for food. Its food includes live animals such as rabbits, squirrels, or snakes. Sometimes the eagle will also eat carrion, or dead animals. The imperial eagle can spot prey from its perch at the top of a tree. It will swoop down and grab the animal in its long, sharp talons, or claws. It uses its talons and beak to kill its prey and tear the food apart.

The eagle hunts not only for itself but also for its young, called eaglets. Eaglets are pure white and fuzzy when they are small. Usually, an eagle lays only one or two eggs. When there are two, one hatches first. The older eaglet often takes more food than the other one. It sometimes even attacks and kills the younger eaglet. So much for getting along in the family!

Males and females share nest duty once the eggs are hatched. They both guard the nest, called an aerie (AIR-ee). And they both hunt for food. Males and females stay together for life, like many other birds do.

At one time Spanish imperial eagles lived in several parts of Europe and Asia. Now they are found mainly in Spain and Portugal. As with many endangered animals, eagles have been harmed the most by humans. In the past, farmers shot them to protect their animals, especially lambs. Eagles also died when they ate poison that was meant for wolves. And, of course, people moved in and took over land where eagles lived. They forced away all the animals so that the eagles had little or no food.

The country of Spain is working to save the imperial eagle. They created a national park where many animals are protected. They also passed a law about the eagles. It says that people may not harm this rare bird in any way.

Color: Black-brown body; patches of white on shoulders; yellow neck and top of head; yellow talons.

WHOOPING CRANE

The killing of the whooping crane made people think. It made them feel guilty. But most of all, it made them take action. In 1945, people in America and Canada realized that their beautiful whooping crane was doomed. There were very few of these birds left in all of North America. And people were killing off the ones that <u>were</u> left. This was the beginning of public education about wildlife. It made the whooping crane the best-known endangered species in North America.

Today there are only about 300 whooping cranes. Some of these live in the wild. Others are in zoos or wildlife centers. Those that live in the wild migrate. They have a winter home and a summer home. From September to March, the cranes live along the Texas Gulf Coast. Then in April the "whoopers" fly to their summer home in Canada. That's a trip of 2,500 miles!

The migration of the whooping cranes has been a problem in the past. A number of birds were often killed along the way. Some died when they flew into electric wires. Sometimes cranes were also killed in storms. But the main threat has always been from hunters. Some people just couldn't resist shooting these huge, graceful birds.

Then there's the story about a farmer who shot 12 whooping cranes at one time. They were eating rice in his field. But the problem was, his farm was once the cranes' habitat, the place where they lived. He had forced them from this habitat by draining the marshes. This left them with no food since cranes eat clams and crabs.

There are also people who don't believe in saving wildlife at all. They feel that most species will die off anyway. One group of farmers in Canada said they would kill every whooping crane they saw. This would put a quick end to the bird. That way we would no longer have to spend money to save it.

Thankfully, there are many people who want to protect whooping cranes. They have passed laws and set aside special land for the birds. They also want to provide safe areas for the cranes while they migrate.

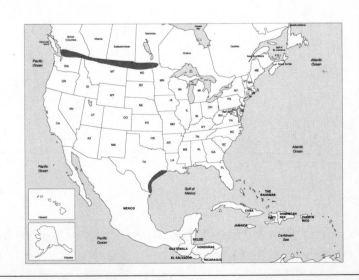

Color: White body; white wings with black edges; red head; pale peach-colored bill nearest the head, darkening to black or dark gray at the tip; and black legs.

SEA OTTER

The sea otter is a water mammal with a rather strange eating habit. It dives deep into the ocean to catch fish or shellfish. Then it comes back to the surface and flips over on its back. It uses its belly as a kind of table for eating, while it floats along on the water. Imagine trying to float and eat at the same time! Sometimes the otter even brings up a stone from the bottom and puts the stone on its chest. It uses the stone to break the shell of the shellfish.

When it comes to floating, the sea otter has a real advantage over you. It has 800 million strands of hair that trap air. The air not only helps the otter float, it also keeps it warm. The air acts as an insulator. This is very helpful because sea otters live in the cold water of the Pacific Ocean. They used to live off of the coast of Japan. They live in the ocean near Washington, California, parts of Canada, and Alaska. The water is very cold that far north.

The sea otter has been hunted for a very long time, almost 3,000 years! When people discovered that the animal's beautiful fur made great coats, they started hunting them even more. In the 126 years that Russia owned Alaska, 800,000 sea otters were killed. As early as 1821 people were trying to do something to save the sea otter. Finally, in 1911 the Fur Seal Treaty was made a law and this protected them.

The sea otter has only a few natural enemies. One is the bald eagle. Another is the great white shark. Humans are still the main enemy of the sea otter, however. The otter gets caught in fishers' nets and can't get out. Also, when people pollute the oceans, this kills the otter because it drinks sea water. And then there's the problem of oil spills in the ocean. This is the worst threat to the sea otter. The oil coats the otter's fur, and destroys the layer of air that insulates it. Then the otter gets waterlogged and drowns.

Many people care about the sea otter. They are trying to provide safe habitats for it. They want it to live in clean, safe waters. They also want to make sure that the sea otter is never again hunted for its fur.

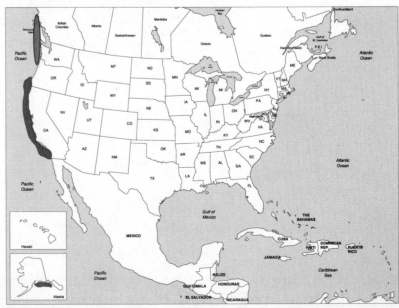

Color: Black or brown with cream-colored throat and chest.

BLACK–FOOTED FERRET

There are many cases where one animal depends on another for its food. Here's a case, though, where one animal depended on another for its food <u>and</u> shelter. When the one was killed off, the other died off in large numbers, too.

The black-footed ferret was once found all over the vast Great Plains of this country. There were hundreds of ferrets. But there weren't nearly as many ferrets as there were prairie dogs. There were billions of these. In fact, there were so many prairie dogs that some places were called prairie dog "towns."

The ferret found out that it liked to eat prairie dogs. It also found that the prairie dog burrow was a good place to live. So when a ferret moved into a prairie dog "town," it thought it had died and gone to heaven. It could have a prairie dog dinner whenever it wanted.

Then along came farmers and ranchers. They hated the prairie dog. This animal made burrows everywhere. It ruined land that was good for farming. It ate grass that ranchers wanted for their livestock. So people started killing the prairie dog. But, as usual, they got carried away. They shot and poisoned the prairie dog in huge numbers. This, of course, killed the black-footed ferret as well. No more prairie dogs meant no more food and no more shelter for the ferret.

Today the black-footed ferret is one of the rarest mammals in the United States. It does not even exist in the wild. There are a few ferrets at a research center in Wyoming, though. There, scientists are raising ferrets. They hope to put the ferret back into its wild habitat some day. A few young ferrets, called kits, have been born at the center. People hope this will continue.

The black-footed ferret is from the weasel family. It grows to a length of one to two feet. It has a long neck and a long, thin body with short legs. It is mainly a night animal that moves quickly to catch its prey. Besides humans, the ferret has other enemies. It is eaten by owls, eagles, and coyotes. At the present time, however, the black-footed ferret is protected from these animals—at least until it is returned to the wild.

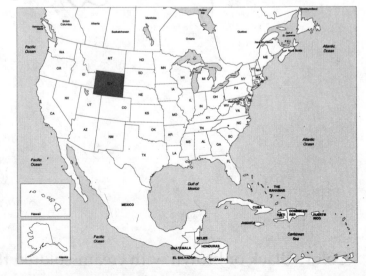

Color: Golden body with dark brown or black feet and end of tail; face has a black "mask" around eyes, and rest of face is white with gold between the ears.

ESKIMO CURLEW

This little bird once migrated from northern Canada to Argentina in South America, every single year. And then, of course, it had to fly back to its breeding ground in Canada. The total trip was about 8,000 miles. This was one of the longest and most dangerous migrations ever recorded!

Why was it so dangerous? For one thing, 4,000 miles one way is very far. Storms sometimes came up. They killed the birds or forced them off course. Hunting, disease, and predation are all partly responsible for killing many of them.

Before long, there were very few Eskimo curlews left. People thought the bird had become extinct. But some have been seen in recent years. In fact, there are so few of them left that scientists have not been able to study a lot of the habits of the curlew. Almost too late this bird is now carefully protected. Scientists are studying current migration routes in order to protect these birds. The curlew is also fully protected by law in the United States and Canada.

Summer Home

Winter Home

Color: Dark brown upper body; light brown below with streaks of dark brown; white or cream-colored throat; black bill; gray-blue legs.

CALIFORNIA CONDOR

Imagine seeing a giant black bird soaring high above you. It glides on the air currents and almost never has to flap its huge wings. It is on the lookout for food far below.

For now, you can only imagine seeing this bird. It is a California condor, which is very rare. It is now extinct in the wild. The only known birds are in special preserves in southern California.

The California condor is one of the largest flying birds in the world. Some weigh from 19 to 22 pounds, which is the size of a small dog. When its wings are spread wide, they measure almost nine feet across. Nine feet would be like putting you and a friend end to end. That's some wingspan!

Now this may surprise you, but the California condor is a kind of vulture. Most people don't think of vultures as being graceful flying birds. They just think that vultures are ugly birds that eat dead animals. But the California condor is a beautiful flying bird. It has sharp eyes and a keen sense of smell. It can find dead deer, rabbits, or cattle from high in the sky. And it has never been known to attack a living creature.

Humans are the only known enemy of the California condor. People have done a lot to harm this bird. They have built too close to its nesting places. They have shot it for its feathers. Ranchers have killed the condor because they thought it would attack their sheep or cattle, even though the condor does not attack living animals.

Poisons have also killed many condors. People put poison on dead animals. They hope this will get rid of coyotes and wolves who eat these animals. But it also kills the condors. Do you know why?

Because so many condors have been killed, there are very few left. And not enough young birds are being born. This is because a male and female condor raise only one young condor every two years. But many people are trying to help the condor. They have set aside areas where it is protected. They have also helped raise condor chicks so the population will grow again.

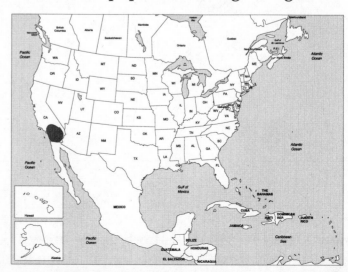

Color: Black body with white under wings; yellow head and red neck, both without feathers.

SNAIL DARTER

The snail darter is a tiny fish that stopped the construction of a big dam-at least for a time. The following time line will show you the events that led to this.

1942   The Tellico Dam Project on the Tennessee River was approved.

1942-1945   The United States was involved in World War II, so people could not work on the dam.

1966   Money was again set aside for the Tellico Dam.

1967   Work was started on the dam.

1973   A professor discovered the snail darter. No one knew it existed before this. The Endangered Species Act became a law.

1975   The snail darter was listed as endangered. People said that building the dam would cause it to become extinct. No darters had been found in any other rivers.

1977   One court said the dam could not be finished.

1978   The Supreme Court (the highest court) also said that the dam could not be completed. They said it would go against the Endangered Species Act.

1979   Congress disagreed with the Supreme Court. They passed a law that said the Tellico Dam must be finished. And so it was.

While all this was going on, scientists tried something to save the snail darter. They put it into other rivers in Tennessee. Many of the snail darters died when this happened. But enough did live to save the fish from becoming extinct.

The snail darter is only about three inches long. It is small enough to hold in one hand. Its name tells a lot about it. It eats mainly snails that live in the water. And it darts after them. The darter, in turn, gets eaten by bigger fish. Those that survive the bigger fish, though, don't live longer than five or six years.

Scientists will continue to watch the snail darter carefully. It seems to be doing well in its current habitat. But water pollution or a lot of building near the river could upset this.

Color: Brown with a trace of green and white below; four dark brown saddle-like patches across the back; head is dark brown and cheeks are mottled brown and yellow.

OREGON SILVERSPOT BUTTERFLY

The Oregon silverspot butterfly got its name for a reason. It is orange and brown with black veins and spots on the back wings; it has a yellow band and bright silver spots on the front wings. And it's obvious where it lives. It is found only in Oregon and Washington along the Pacific Coast. Here the weather is mild but moist. There is much rain and fog.

Here, too, is found the western blue violet. This plant is very important to the Oregon silverspot. It is a host plant for the butterfly's eggs. In late August, the female butterfly lays about 200 or more eggs near the western blue violet. This plant is chosen because it will supply food for the eggs. A sticky fluid around the eggs holds them to the plant.

An egg will hatch in about 16 days. It is then a larva, or caterpillar. The caterpillar finds a place to spend the winter. In spring, it eats the leaves of the western blue violet for about two months. That's all a caterpillar does—it eats and grows. It grows larger and larger. Soon it gets too large for its skin. Then the skin splits and comes off. When the caterpillar has reached full size, it turns into a pupa. It continues in this stage for about two to three weeks.

During this third stage, a hard shell forms over the pupa. The greatest changes of all take place at this time. The caterpillar changes into a butterfly.

The whole process that the butterfly goes through is called metamorphosis (met-uh-MOR-foh-sis).

1. Egg   2. Larva (Caterpillar) 3. Pupa   4. Adult

The building of homes and recreational use of the land are the biggest threats to the Oregon silverspot. This upsets its habitat. It also destroys the western blue violet, which is so important to the butterfly. People have worked together in Oregon to preserve the silverspot's habitat. They prepared a Habitat Conservation Plan. They also set aside a special area where many of the butterflies and violets can exist together.

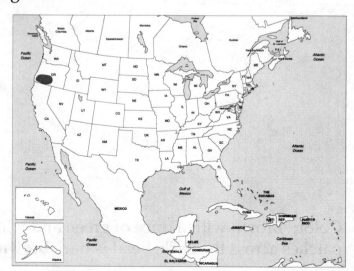

Color: Orange and brown with black veins and spots on back wings; yellow band and silver spots on front wings.

TOOTH CAVE SPIDER

The Tooth Cave spider is found in one place and one place only—Tooth Cave. This cave is near the city of Austin, Texas. It is not known just how many tiny Tooth Cave spiders live here. But because this is the only place where this spider exists and because the cave itself is endangered, the spider is endangered, too.

Tooth Cave was formed out of limestone. Limestone is a rock that can be slowly dissolved (or eaten away) by water and carbon dioxide. The water and carbon dioxide make a weak acid. This acid water gets into cracks in the rock. Over thousands of years, the water hollows out tunnels. These tunnels later become caves.

Tooth Cave is located in a bad place—at least for the <u>cave</u>. It is near a growing community. People want to spread out from Austin. They want to build homes and shopping malls and suburbs. And Tooth Cave just doesn't fit in with the suburbs. One major problem is that heavy digging equipment is used in building. This can damage Tooth Cave and weaken its structure. This can cause the cave to "cave in." And you know what that would do to all living things in the cave, including the Tooth Cave spider.

The tiny Tooth Cave spider has fairly long legs, but its body is only about 1/10 inch long. It eats insects that live in the cave or happen to wander in. The spider spins webs on the walls and ceilings of the cave. These silky webs catch the insects for the spider to eat. And why doesn't the spider get caught in its own web? It has a special oil on its body. This keeps the silk from sticking to the spider.

The spider and a few other animal species in Tooth Cave are now on the Endangered Animal list. This will cause people to look more carefully at Tooth Cave itself as an endangered habitat.

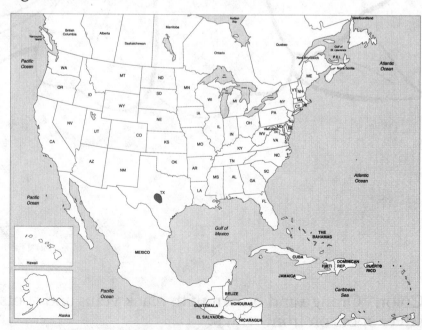

Color: See-through peach.

AMERICAN BURYING BEETLE

To many people, a big black bug is just another bug—probably a pest. But insects are on the endangered species list, too.

The American burying beetle was once found in 32 states and some places in Canada. It is now known to be in only two areas. One place is a small island just off the coast of Massachusetts. The other is in eastern Oklahoma. Scientists tell us that no other insect has ever died off in such great numbers as the American burying beetle.

Why did this happen? Some people think that DDT, a chemical used to kill insects, killed this beetle in great numbers. DDT is no longer used to kill harmful insects. This is because it was very strong and lasted for several years. It was blamed for killing hundreds of birds, fish, and other wildlife.

"Bug zappers" have also killed off many of the burying beetles. The "zappers," which are popular for killing mosquitoes, kill other insects as well. They attract the males and then basically burn them to death. Without males, the beetle population cannot increase.

The name beetle means "biter." Most beetles have very strong jaws. They use these jaws for catching and chewing their food.

The American burying beetle is a shiny black beetle about one inch long. It has special red and orange markings. It is known by two names—the American burying beetle and the giant carrion beetle. It has both of these names for a reason. This beetle finds its food by smell. And most of its food is carrion, or dead insects. Several beetles will fight with each other for this food. Then the winner takes the food and buries it in moist soil. Sometimes the burying beetle will also capture live insects. What do you think the beetle does with these?

To protect the American burying beetle, scientists are still studying its current habitat, the place where it lives. They are also keeping the exact location of this beetle a secret. They don't want people to capture and collect this rare insect.

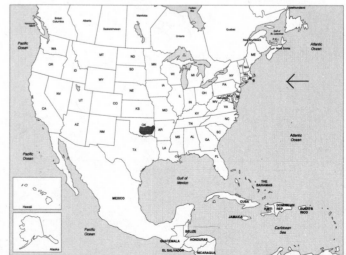

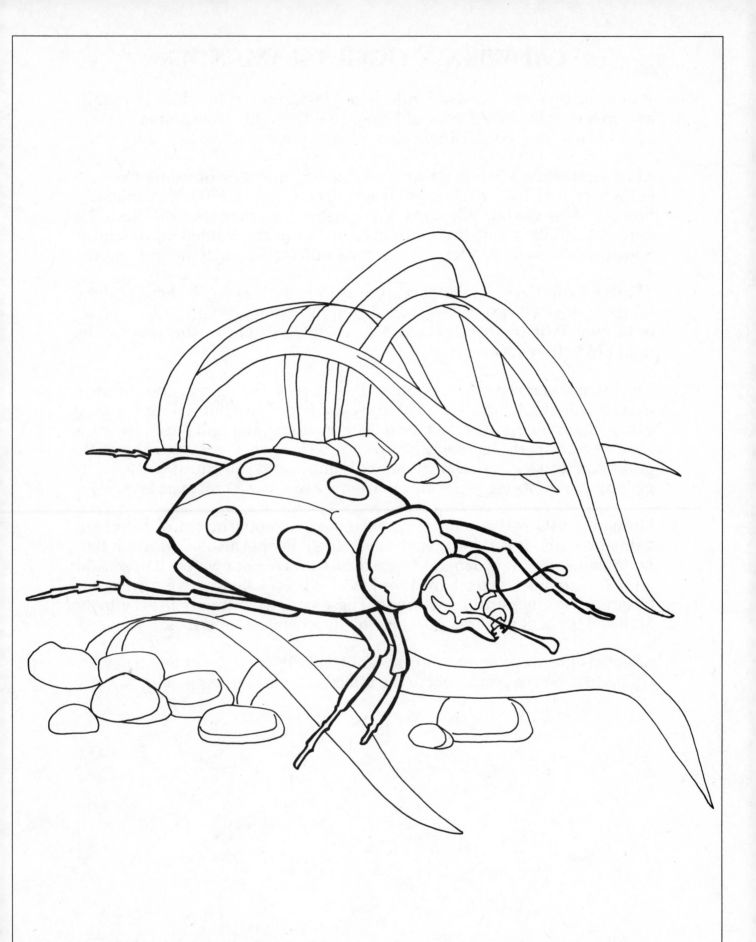

Color: Black body with red spots on back; red antennae with orange tips; orange-red "disk" behind head.

CALIFORNIA TIGER SALAMANDER

When you first look at a salamander, would you guess it is in the same family as a frog or a lizard? If you said <u>frog</u>, you are right. This animal is cold-blooded and has moist, slimy skin. A lizard tends to have dry, scaly skin.

Most salamanders live in streams and ponds, in caves, or under stones—anywhere it is cool, dark, and damp. The California tiger salamander, however, lives in a fairly dry area. You can see on the map where it lives. This part of California gets little rain except during the winter rainy season. Sometimes this salamander will burrow around lakes and temporary ponds.

The California tiger salamander can be up to 13 inches long. Its head is round with small eyes. It varies in colors and patterns. Some are black, olive, yellow, or brown. With this kind of coloring, where do you think this salamander might hide from its enemies?

The salamander is a harmless animal—except to the worms and insects it eats. It will usually run and hide to escape an enemy. But it if can't hide, it can do other things to protect itself. For one thing, it might be able to grow new limbs, or parts, like some lizards do. So if an enemy (such as a person) grabs hold of a leg, the salamander will squirm and squirm. It will actually give up part of its leg to get away. Then it can grow a new part later.

Humans are the main enemy of the salamander. People hunt and collect this animal because it is colorful and interesting. People also kill it when they build dams. Building dams changes the natural flow of water. It upsets the animal's balance. The salamander has also been killed by polluted water. Chemicals get into streams or ponds. These same chemicals then get into the animal's flesh. It becomes poisoned by the chemicals and dies.

Scientists are working to help the California tiger salamander. They are trying to preserve ponds where the salamander lays its eggs.

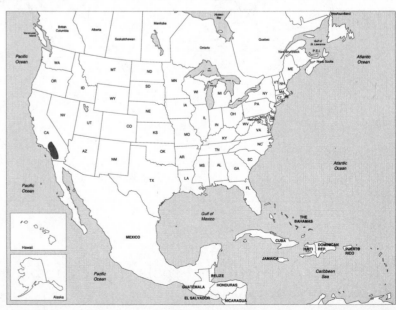

Color: Can vary from black, brown, olive, or yellow.

GALAPAGOS PENGUIN

Some interesting and rare animals live on the Galapagos (guh-LAH-puh-gus) Islands. These islands are in the Pacific Ocean west of the country of Ecuador in South America. Here are found rare hawks and weird sea birds called "boobies." There are also two kinds of birds that cannot fly. And there are huge turtles that weigh more than 500 pounds. In fact, the islands are named for these turtles. "Galapagos" is the Spanish word for turtle.

The Galapagos penguin is one of the birds that cannot fly. It probably had wings about a million years ago, but it has since lost its ability to fly. It may have been that its ancestors had an easy life. Perhaps they had few enemies, so they no longer needed wings to fly away. Their wings, then, developed into flippers.

The flippers and the penguin's webbed feet make it a great swimmer and diver. It may waddle funny while on land, but in the water, the penguin is very graceful. Its short, thick feathers also help it in the water. They give it a waterproof coat. This coat, along with thick layers of fat, keep the penguin warm in cold water.

Penguins live south of the Equator. Many are found in the cold, cold Antarctic. Others live around New Zealand, Australia, and South Africa. So what are some penguins doing as far north as the Galapagos Islands? These islands are almost near the Equator. The reason is that the cool waters of the Humboldt current reach that far north. Penguins probably followed those currents in the past and settled on the Galapagos Islands. These currents also bring food to the penguins.

Between May and July the penguins hatch their young. They make nests of stones in a cave or crevice on the coast. Only two eggs are laid in the nest.

Color: Dark brown or black with white front.

MANATEE

At first glance, the manatee, or sea cow, may look like a chubby whale with the face of a walrus. But it is not even closely related to cows, whales, or walruses. Its nearest relative is the elephant! So where's the trunk?, you might ask. And why doesn't it walk on land?

Perhaps long ago, an animal like this lived on land and in the water. It ate both land and water plants. Now, however, this animal is so adapted to water that it cannot live on land at all. And it is no longer anything like an elephant.

The manatee may be about ten feet long and weigh close to 2,000 pounds (that's a ton!). It spends a good part of its day looking for and eating plants. And this animal is a serious eater. It may eat up to 100 pounds of plants a day.

The manatee does not have a thick layer of fat to keep it warm. Therefore, it lives in warm water. This animal is found mainly in the coastal waters from Florida to Brazil. Changes in water temperature can kill the manatee, especially the young ones.

Humans are the only enemy of the manatee. In the past, people killed the animal for its hide, its oil, and its meat. Hunting is now illegal. But the manatee is sometimes killed by motor boats as it searches for food near the surface of the water. Boaters don't see the animal and run right over it.

People have raised a lot of money to help save the manatee. They have also passed laws about boating in areas where the animal lives.

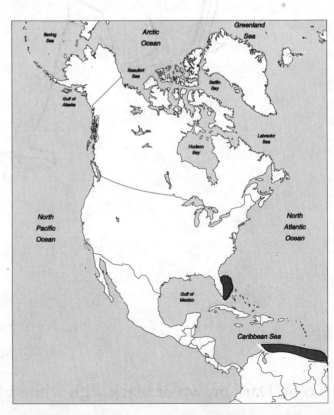

Color: Light to dark gray.

GIANT ANTEATER

Before you start to read about the giant anteater, get a ruler or yardstick and measure off 24 inches. Or just estimate this length. (This sheet of paper is about 11 inches from top to bottom.) Got the length measured or in mind?

Twenty-four inches is the length of the giant anteater's <u>tongue.</u> This long, wet tongue can scoop out lots of ants or termites each day. The anteater doesn't bother to chew the insects. It just swallows them whole. Then they are ground up by the muscles in its stomach.

The anteater finds all these insects by sniffing. In fact, it sniffs almost constantly. As you might guess, it has a very good sense of smell. When it finds an anthill or a termite nest, the anteater uses the claws on its forepaws. These claws are curved and very sharp. They can open even the hardest termite nest. The anteater then uses its long snout to make the opening larger. When that's done, it goes to work with its long tongue.

Besides having an odd-looking snout, the anteater is rather odd-looking all over. It is a large mass of black-brown hair with a big, bushy tail. It can swim if it needs to—even across wide rivers. If attacked, the anteater will use its very strong arms and claws. It can stand up on its back legs and throw its arms around the enemy. Then it will dig its sharp claws into the other animal's hide. It doesn't always win, but at least it can defend itself.

The giant anteater lives in grasslands and forests. It is found in South America. Its numbers are few. It is protected by law in some places, but people still shoot it. Many people are afraid of the anteater, even though it does not harm humans.

Other threats, of course, are the fact that people hunt them a lot and take over their habitat. People destroy the anteater's habitat when they cut down trees. Giant anteaters are protected by law in Brazil and French Guiana.

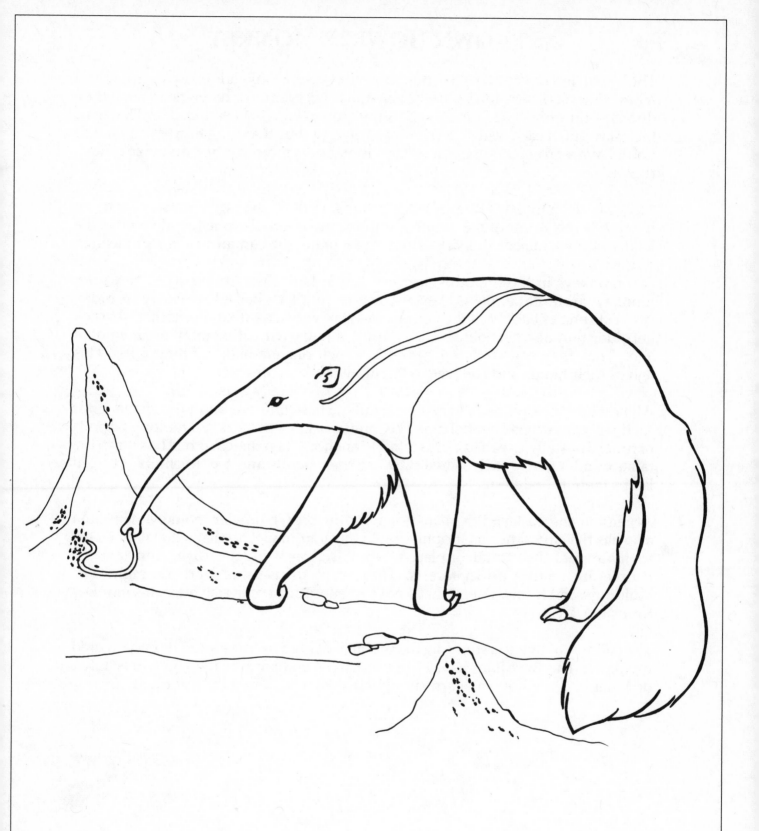

Color: Black-brown or gray-brown body with white and black-brown markings and a dark brown-black tail.

BROWN HOWLER MONKEY

The brown howler monkey has this name for two reasons. It is brown in color and it howls. It has a very loud voice. Each morning, groups of howlers do what they do best—they howl. This lets neighboring groups know where they are. That way, they stay out of each others' territories. You might be thankful, however, that you don't have a group of howler monkeys living next to <u>you</u>. They do make quite a racket!

Most howler monkeys live in large groups. One of the adult males, often the biggest, is the leader of the whole group. There is usually one female who is the leader of the females. But since she is not a male, she cannot be the main leader.

The monkeys in these groups are very gentle with their young ones. Newborn monkeys are quite helpless. They rest on their mother's belly. When they are older, they ride on her back. But the young ones stay very close to their mother. As they get older, they also get bolder. They go out and play with other monkeys their own age. They may have fighting games in which players hang by their tails. This leaves their hands and feet free to "fight" with each other.

All howler monkeys have very strong tails. These tails are like a fifth hand since their feet can serve as hands, too. The monkeys hang by their tail for long periods of time. They also use their tail as a safety anchor when they climb. They wrap the tail around a tree branch. Then they use their hands and feet to climb. The tail keeps them from falling.

Argentina and eastern Brazil are home for the brown howler monkey. This area also has the largest human population in that country. And that's the main threat to this animal. Its habitat, or place where it lives, is being destroyed almost daily. People are cutting down forests. They want to use this land for highways, buildings, and farms. And if that's not bad enough, people also hunt this monkey for its meat.

The country of Brazil is studying the problem of both its forests and its endangered monkeys. The Brazilians have built a research center for the monkeys. It is in Rio de Janeiro. They hope to learn enough to save this animal from extinction.

Color: Black-brown body.

These organizations are all working to help preserve animals and the places they need to live. You can write to them to find out what you can do to help or to ask for more information about one of the animals you have read about in this book or in other books. Ask your parents for permission to call any of these groups.

Greenpeace USA
1436 U Street
Washington, D.C. 20009
(202) 462-1177

National Audubon Society
950 Third Avenue
New York, New York 10022
(212) 546-9100

National Wildlife Federation
1400 16th Street, NW
Washington, D.C. 20036
(202) 797-6800

**Natural Resources
Defense Council**
40 West 20th Street
New York, New York 10011
(212) 727-2700

The Nature Conservancy
1815 North Lynn Street
Arlington, Virginia 22209
(703) 841-5300

Sierra Club
Public Affairs Department
730 Polk Street
San Francisco, California 94109
(415) 923-5660

Wilderness Society
900 17th Street, NW
Washington, D.C. 20006
(202) 833-2300

**World Wildlife Fund/
Conservation Foundation**
1250 24th Street, NW
Suite 400
Washington, D.C. 20037
(202) 293-4800